THE
QUOTABLE
CANINE

THE
QUOTABLE
CANINE

PETOGRAPHY INC.

Jim Dratfield and Paul Coughlin

PHOTOGRAPHY BY PAUL COUGHLIN
ART DIRECTION BY JIM DRATFIELD

DOUBLEDAY

NEW YORK   LONDON   TORONTO   SYDNEY   AUCKLAND

PUBLISHED BY DOUBLEDAY
a division of Bantam Doubleday Dell
Publishing Group, Inc.
1540 Broadway, New York, New York 10036

DOUBLEDAY and the portrayal of an anchor
with a dolphin are trademarks of Doubleday, a
division of Bantam Doubleday Dell Publishing
Group, Inc.

Book design by Marysarah Quinn

Library of Congress Cataloging-in-Publication
Data
Dratfield, Jim.
The quotable canine / Jim Dratfield &
Paul Coughlin. — 1st ed.
p.   cm.
1. Dogs—Pictorial works. 2. Dogs—
Quotations, maxims, etc. I. Coughlin,
Paul. II. Title.
SF430.D73   1995
636.7′00207—dc20   94-31818
                                              CIP
ISBN 0-385-47554-3
Copyright © 1995 by Jim Dratfield and
Paul Coughlin
All Rights Reserved
Printed in Hong Kong
September 1995
First Edition

1   3   5   7   9   10   8   6   4   2

To Paradise Walnut
Jones and Kuma the
Wonderdog for being
our inspiration, to
Donald Williams for
being "the glue," and to
Virginia Bell for being
our "fifth business."

The authors wish to thank
Lee Dratfield, Susan Golomb,
Carol Hyatt, and Jerry Sheehan
for their support.

For their help with production
we thank Michelle Fichera, Marti
Anderson, Zeke Martin, Manuel
Tamayo, Razzmatazz Chinese
Cresteds, and the Flash team:
Joe and Sam.

In addition, grateful
acknowledgment is made to
Mary Ann Crenshaw, Dominique
Davis, Amy Fernandez,
No Standing Anytime Ltd.,
Carol Nolan, Carl Bielby, Joyce
Denebrink, Fern Michaels, Jane
Kronick, Judy Yee, Joy Handler,
Brandon Saltz, Joyce O'Neil, Robin
Kovary, Elizabeth Kathryn Pugh,
Jerry Scarano, Carl Heit, Bunky
Runser, and a special
thank-you to our editor,
Judy Kern.

Faithful unto Death

With eye upraised his
master's look to scan,
The joy, the solace, and
the aid of man:
The rich man's
guardian and the poor
man's friend,
The only creature
faithful to the end.

—George Crabbe

In loving memory—
Kuma the Wonderdog

October 10,1984–December 4, 1994

THE
QUOTABLE
CANINE

A door is what a dog
is perpetually on the
wrong side of.

—OGDEN NASH

Both humans and dogs love to play well into adulthood, and individuals from both species occasionally display evidence of having a conscience.

—JON WINOKUR,
CONTEMPORARY AMERICAN WRITER

The more I know
of men, the more
I love my dog.

—Madame de Sévigné

Oh, what is
the matter with
poor Puggy-wug?
Pet him and kiss him
and give him a hug.
Run and fetch him
a suitable drug.
Wrap him up
tenderly all in a rug.
That is the way to
cure Puggy-wug.

—WINSTON CHURCHILL
ON HIS DAUGHTER MARY'S PET PUG

I know that dogs
are pack animals,
but it's difficult to
imagine a pack of
standard poodles …
and if there was such
a thing as a pack of
standard poodles where
would they rove to?
Bloomingdales?

—YVONNE CLIFFORD,
AMERICAN ACTRESS

The great pleasure
of a dog is that you
make a fool of yourself
with him and not only
will he not scold you,
he will make a fool
of himself too.

—SAMUEL BUTLER

The pug is living
proof that God has
a sense of humor.

—Margo Kaufman,
American writer

Me thinks I am
marvellous hairy
about the face.

—WILLIAM SHAKESPEARE,
A MIDSUMMER NIGHT'S DREAM

Outside of a dog,
a man's best friend
is a book; inside of a
dog, it's very dark.

—Groucho Marx

M y little dog—a
heartbeat at my feet.

—Edith Wharton

She had no
particular breed
in mind, no unusual
requirements. Except
the special sense of
mutual recognition
that tells dog and
human they have both
come to the right place.

—LLOYD ALEXANDER,
AMERICAN WRITER

The poor dog, in life
the firmest friend,
The first to welcome,
foremost to defend.

—Lord Byron,

an epitaph for his dog,

Boatswain

A good dog never dies
he always stays
he walks beside you
on crisp autumn days
when frost is on the fields
and winter's drawing near
his head is within our hand
in his old way.

—MARY CAROLYN DAVIES

Children and dogs
are as necessary to
the welfare of the
country as Wall Street
and the railroads.

—Harry S. Truman

God . . . sat down
for a moment when
the dog was finished
in order to watch it . . .
and to know that it was
good, that nothing
was lacking, that it
could not have been
made better.

—RAINER MARIA RILKE

If a dog's prayers were answered, bones would rain from the sky.

—OLD PROVERB

A dog is like
an eternal Peter Pan,
a child who never
grows old and who
therefore is always
available to love
and be loved.

—AARON KATCHER,
AMERICAN EDUCATOR
AND PSYCHIATRIST

She was such
a beautiful and
sweet creature . . .
and so full of tricks.

—QUEEN VICTORIA

Properly trained,
a man can be dog's
best friend.

—COREY FORD,
AMERICAN WRITER

W hat kind of life
a dog . . . acquires,
I have sometimes tried
to imagine by kneeling
or lying full length on
the ground and looking
up. The world then
becomes strangely
incomplete: one sees
little but legs.

—E. V. Lucas,
English writer

Fifth Avenue is
too expensive for
anyone but dogs.

—Mel Finkelstein,
Daily News

My dog can bark
like a congressman,
fetch like an aide,
beg like a press
secretary, and play
dead like a receptionist
when the phone rings.

—GERALD SOLOMON,
UNITED STATES CONGRESSMAN

H<small>ERE</small>, Gentlemen,
a dog teaches us a
lesson in humanity.

—N<small>APOLEON</small> B<small>ONAPARTE</small>

They never talk
about themselves but
listen to you while you
talk about yourself, and
keep up an appearance
of being interested in
the conversation.

—JEROME K. JEROME,
ENGLISH HUMORIST

Not Carnegie,
Vanderbilt and Astor
together could have
raised money enough
to buy a quarter share
in my little dog . . .

—ERNEST THOMPSON SETON,
AMERICAN WRITER AND NATURALIST

Acquiring a dog may be the only opportunity a human ever has to choose a relative.

—MORDECAI SIEGAL,
CONTEMPORARY WRITER

Being patted is
what it is all about.

—ROGER CARAS

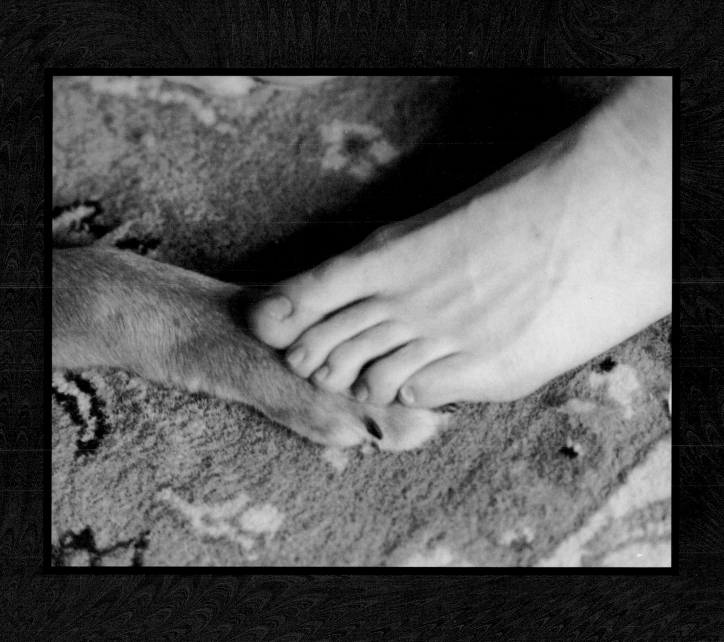

The Saluki . . .
is a marvel of elegance.

—Vita Sackville-West

A naked dog
for a naked lady.

—ATTRIBUTED TO
GYPSY ROSE LEE

Bulldogs are adorable, with faces like toads that have been sat on.

—COLETTE

My hounds are bred
out of the spartan kind;
So flew'd, so sanded;
their heads are hung
With ears that sweep
away the morning dew . . .

—WILLIAM SHAKESPEARE,
A Midsummer Night's Dream

Some dogs live for praise
they look at you as if to say
"Don't throw balls . . .
just throw bouquets."

—JHORDIS ANDERSEN,
AMERICAN PAINTER

He was vain,
even arrogant,
he was splendid,
magnanimous,
noble, he was utterly
superb . . . the fact
that he lived at all was a
blessing and a miracle.

—Roger Caras

Sir, this is a unique
dog. He does not live
by tooth or fang. He
respects the right of
cats to be cats although
he doesn't admire them.
He turns his steps
rather than disturb
an earnest caterpillar.
His greatest fear is that
someone will point out
a rabbit and suggest
that he chase it. This is
a dog of peace and
tranquility.

—JOHN STEINBECK

Dogs are our link
to paradise. They don't
know evil or jealousy
or discontent. To sit
with a dog on a hillside
on a glorious afternoon
is to be back in Eden,
where doing nothing
was not boring—
it was peace.

—MILAN KUNDERA

Why is it that my heart is so touched whenever I meet a dog lost in our noisy streets? Why do I feel such anguished pity when I see one of these creatures coming and going, sniffing everyone, frightened, despairing of even finding its master?

—Emile Zola

They are better
than human beings,
because they know
but do not tell.

—Emily Dickinson

In the late summer afternoon, when the tea cups were cleared, and the family went inside . . . the dogs, who are no longer under human command, find delight in the company of each other.

—JOE DUNNEA,
IRISH WRITER

The airedale . . .
an unrivaled mixture
of brains and clownish
wit, the very ingredients
one looks for in a spouse.

—Chip Brown,
Connoisseur magazine

His name is not
wild dog anymore,
but the first friend,
because he will be our
friend for always and
always and always.

—Rudyard Kipling

LIST OF PHOTOGRAPHS

Paul Coughlin grew up in a small New Jersey shore town where he first developed a love of photography. He moved to New York to pursue a theatrical career, but found he was still in love with taking pictures. Mr. Coughlin prefers traditional, sepia-toned black and white photography for its distinctive, gentle, other-era quality.

"There are little things around us that tell us where we've been. I often wonder if, years from now, someone will find one of my photos and wonder about this beautiful dog that lived in the 1990s."

Jim Dratfield is from Princeton, New Jersey. He spent fourteen years as an actor, working on various projects including the Broadway revival of *The Man Who Came to Dinner* and the recurring role of Bud Keiser on the television series "St. Elsewhere." As a producer, Jim's O. Drat! Productions earned acclaim for its award-winning production of Lanford Wilson's *Fifth of July*. His love for animals and photography has led to his co-creation, with Paul Coughlin, of Petography, a company specializing in fine-art photographic animal portraiture, for which he is the art director.